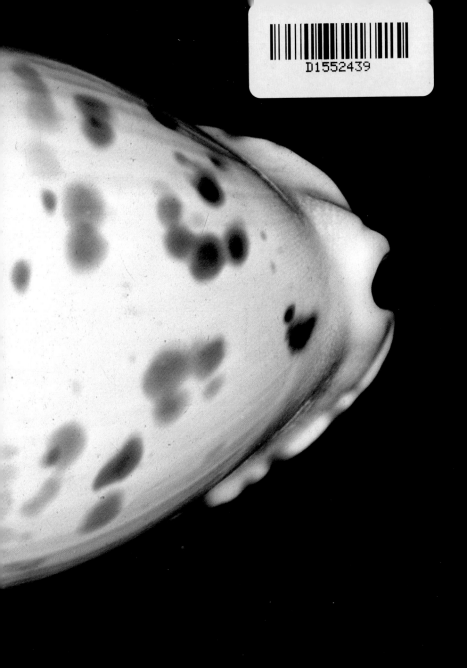

Contents:
WHY COLLECT? ... 6; THE COLLECTION ... 18; NOW THE
SHELLS ... 46; READING IS FUNDAMENTAL ... 64; THE ENVI-
RONMENTAL QUESTION ... 82.

Color photos by K. Gillett are from the books *Australian Seashores
in Colour* and *The Australian Great Barrier Reef in Colour,* both
published by A.H. & A.W. Reed, Sydney, Australia.

COVERS: Some common Australian shells. Photos by K. Gillett.
ENDPAPERS: *Cypraea marginata.* Photo by W. Deas.
TITLE PAGE: The joys of collecting shells. Photo by Leslie Easland.

Acknowledgments

When I started collecting shells several years ago, I made my share of mistakes
and met my share of poor or simply bad dealers, but it took little time to realize
that in the maze of shops and dealers were some that were much better than the
rest. Due to circumstances leading to the writing of three family-level shell
books, I've perhaps seen a side of shell dealers not seen by most collectors. I can
only say that to: Bob Morrison, Sarasota, Florida; Dick Kurz, Wauwatosa,
Wisconsin; M.E. Young, Falls Church, Virginia; and Bob and Dottie Janowsky,
Brooklyn, New York, can be traced some of my most pleasurable moments in
collecting. May all collectors, at all levels, have similar moments that are as
much the essence of shell collecting as the shells.

My special thanks also to Dr. Warren E. Burgess for his help and suggestions
in this and many other shell projects, and to Maleta for her continuing en-
couragement.

t.f.h.

© 1981 T.F.H. Publications, Inc. Ltd.

ISBN 0-87666-631-4

Distributed in the U.S. by T.F.H. Publications, Inc., 211 West Sylvania Avenue, PO Box
427, Neptune, NJ 07753; in England by T.F.H. (Gt. Britain) Ltd., 13 Nutley Lane, Reigate,
Surrey; in Canada to the pet trade by Rolf C. Hagen Ltd., 3225 Sartelon Street, Montreal
382, Quebec; in Southeast Asia by Y.W. Ong, 9 Lorong 36 Geylang, Singapore 14; in
Australia and the South Pacific by Pet Imports Pty. Ltd., P.O. Box 149, Brookvale 2100,
N.S.W. Australia; in South Africa by Valid Agencies, P.O. Box 51901, Randburg 2125
South Africa. Published by T.F.H. Publications, Inc., Ltd, the British Crown Colony of
Hong Kong.

SHELL COLLECTING

BY JERRY G. WALLS

Left: An exquisite *Cypraea marginata* posed on a tulip and photographed by Dr. Herbert R. Axelrod.

Right: Many marine invertebrates, including molluscs, seek darkness and shelter under coral boulders. Photo by K. Gillett.

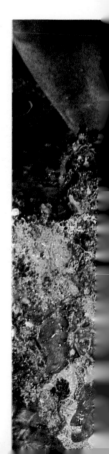

Why Collect?

Shells are merely sophisticated calcium deposits riding on the backs of snails, clams, and a few other molluscs. When coarsely crushed they make passable road surfaces, and when finely ground they are excellent additions to chicken feed. Yet these easily broken structures have attracted man's attention for literally thousands of years, first as objects of religious superstition or ceremonial appliances, then as valuable cabinet pieces in private museums of the middle ages, and finally as the basis of the popularized science of conchology, the study of shells. (Malacology is the more formal study of both the shell and soft parts of snails, clams, squids, and other molluscs that may or may not form a shell—in other words, the mollusc in its entirety. For the purposes of this book we are concerned with only the dead shell after it leaves the mollusc that formed it.)

There is no completely explainable reason for this attraction between some people and shells, no more than there is an obvious reason why some people collect stamps or Hummel figurines. The attraction simply exists and, if allowed to grow, leads to the production of a conchologist. Most budding conchologists obtain their first shells with no prior intention of becoming collectors. They pick up a worn, worm-ridden shell on their vacation to the shore, are given a shell as a gift by a well-meaning friend, or wander into a shell curio shop to pick up a set of napkin rings or the "cute little turtle" made from shells. The initial contact leads to a casual look at a few other cheap shells and the obvious questions—"Who painted them?" and "What did they polish them with?"

If you are at this level, then hopefully this book will help guide you into shell collecting and will help you discover ways of enjoying your hobby to the fullest. Like all hobbies, shell collecting has its good and bad points, its joys and its pains. As long as you remember that it is just a hobby, however, and exists just for fun, you should enjoy your shells. A hobby is for relaxation; don't take it too seriously.

COLLECTORS

Once you have decided that shells are appealing to you, you have several different possibilities open: you may be a casual collector (barely a true collector in my opinion), a general collector, or a specialist collector. Perhaps most collectors are first casual collectors before evolving into more scientific collectors.

There is nothing wrong with a casual collection of shells. *Casual collectors* pick up basically shells that are interesting to them because of their beauty, unusual form, or some personal attachment. Casual collectors usually are satisfied with—or even prefer—shells that have been treated with acids and shellac to enhance their colors and gloss. They don't mind a few broken spines on a murex, a chipped lip on a cone, or a nacre flaw on a cowry. They prefer larger, oddly shaped shells that look nice on the coffee table or bookcase. Scientific names are unnecessary for their collecting enjoyment because they buy only in person at curio shops or at the beach.

It seems likely to me, although there are probably no statistics to prove it, that casual collectors form the majority of all shell collectors. This would seem to be borne out by the very large number of commercial grade shells sold each year—after all, there is many times more of a market for a $1 tiger cowry than for small miters or cones that sell for the same dollar. The quantity of shells sold at beach-front curio stands is obviously gigantic and involves more pieces than are handled by even large specimen-shell dealers. So who can argue with success?

Actually, the shells purchased by casual collectors often cost more than equivalent shells purchased from specimen-shell dealers. This is because specimen-shell dealers have to sell to collectors who know something about relative scarcity of shells and their market value. A casual collector is likely to spend $5 for a badly flawed mole cowry *(Cypraea talpa)* that a more advanced collector wouldn't give $1 for.

The only real problem with the casual collector is that it is so easy for him to never really learn anything about the shells. The casual collector seldom purchases a book, never worries about where the shell really came from, and the possibility that much more fascinating shells exist never enters his mind. The shell on the shelf is the beginning and the end of his hobby.

The *general collector* has advanced greatly over the casual collector, though there are still similarities. He is happy with almost any shell he can get, regardless of its source. Thus a general collection might contain not only a good showing of the more common or attractive cowries, cones, murexes, volutes, conchs, and bursas, but also samples of smaller groups such as miters, marginellas, whelks, pectens, clams, and even a few land snails. Shells are obtained through purchase, trade, and self-collecting as opportunities arise, with an eye on making as large and diverse a collection as possible, the ultimate goal (unreachable of course) being to have one or two of every shell species.

I'm not at all sure that the general collector isn't the wisest of the three collecting types. After all, he is in the enviable position of being able to "spread himself thin," remaining interested in *all* shells. Unlike the casual collector, the general collector must be at least somewhat involved with literature and identifications, but doesn't have to be as identification-conscious as the specialist. The shells are more available to him, as good

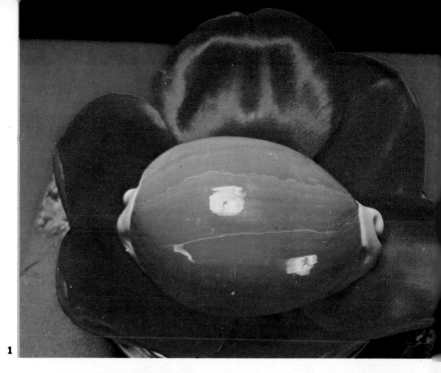

1

Almost every shell family has extremes of value and desirability. For instance, the golden cowry pictured above (1) is a choice collector's item no matter what its condition, while the tiger cowry is abundant enough to be cut into napkin rings (2). Photos by Dr. Herbert R. Axelrod. Opposite: A display of shells (3) in a dealer's shop can be both thrilling and frustrating—no collector can obtain every shell he desires. Photo by Dr. Herbert R. Axelrod at the Collector's Cabinet, New York.

2

1

Cowries such as *Cypraea argus* (1) are favorites with collectors, while bivalves (2) seldom interest anyone unless they are colorful or heavily ornamented. Photo 2 by G. Marcuse.

2

specimens of great interest can be found by self-collecting on any shore vacation, by carefully picking through the stock of a curio shop, by friendly trades with pals in other countries, and by purchasing from the lists of dealers. Once a group has gone beyond his financial means (after all, every major collectable shell group has some or many expensive species), he can focus attention on the next group of interest. In this way a large and very representative collection can be formed rather cheaply over a period of years.

Offhand, I really can't think of any major disadvantages with general collecting, other than it requires a large amount of room to store such a large collection. On a psychological level, specialists tend to look down on general collectors for some reason, which could affect his ego if the general collector becomes involved with shell clubs. Perhaps specialists have become so involved in their small groups that some tend to think of non-specialists as rather "childish" and not very advanced. Actually, general collectors are often among the best-informed collectors and the happiest in their hobby. Also, most specialists started out as general collectors and later decided that one or two families were of greater interest than the rest. So don't feel "put down" if you are a general collector.

The last group of collectors is that of the specialists. The *specialist collector* is interested in collecting every species and variety from as many localities as possible in only one or two groups of shells, usually larger families such as cones, cowries, pectens, miters, etc. The specialist may have started as a general collector and then become involved in a single family for some obscure reason even he couldn't explain. Thus some people find murexes beautiful shells, while I personally find them delicate, expensive, colorless, and hard to store; I have absolutely no interest in collecting murexes. I like cones, but many collectors feel cones are dull, cumbersome, incredibly hard to identify, and over-priced. To each his own—there is no stigma attached to specializing in any group.

The specialist collector considers himself the cream of collectors, perhaps rightly so. By specializing in one or a very few groups, it is possible to see the entire development of a family rather than just the larger or cheaper species. The specialist in

1

An assortment of cowries, genus *Cypraea.* 1) (top to bottom): *C. asellus, C. helvola, C. staphylaea, C. cribraria, Calpurnus verrucosus* (an allied cowry), *C. annulus,* and *C. moneta.* Photo by K. Gillett. 2) *Cypraea capensis,* an endemic South African species. 3) *Cypraea langfordi,* a rare and attractive species. 4) *Cypraea diluculum,* a common but attractive East African species. 5 & 6) Ventral and dorsal views of *Cypraea leucodon,* perhaps the rarest and most expensive cowry.

2

3

4

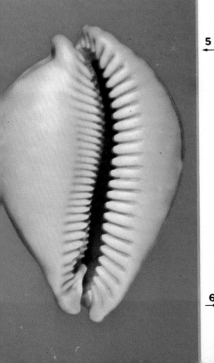

5

6

The history of some shells is almost as interesting as the shells themselves. *Conus dusaveli,* shown here in a photograph by T.C. Good, was described in 1872 from a unique specimen found in the stomach of a fish supposedly taken off the island of Mauritius. It was not seen again until specimens were taken in Okinawa and the Philippines in the middle 1970's, and so far no other specimens have been found in the Indian Ocean, let alone Mauritius. The species is now available in numbers but still sells in the $1,000-range.

the major families of course is unlikely to ever complete his family because of financial considerations, virtually unobtainable species, and often confused systematics. Thus even the richest cone collector will be missing at least one or two rare species and will be uncertain as to whether he really has some of the more doubtful species or not.

Of necessity, the specialist collector is heavily dependent on other specialists, museums, dealers, and specialized literature. He cannot exist for long without the latest revisions and new species descriptions. Each new dealer's list is anxiously scanned not only for species not in the collection, but also for specimens from new locations or representing unusual varieties. Many specialists become so involved in their group as to have strong opinions on identification and are willing to share them in articles in club journals.

However, there are numerous problems involved in the specialist collection. The first is money. To come close to completing a major family a great deal of money is necessary eventually. Even if you self-collect extensively, there are always species that you cannot personally collect and that are too expensive to be affordable even through trades. Another problem is that of the shells I call "tag alongs." Every family has its share of unattractive and uninteresting species that must be obtained and stored for completion of the collection. Although no two collectors of a family would agree on which species are the "tag alongs," they all must acknowledge that some species are barely worth storage room, let alone the time and expense.

Of necessity, the specialist must have at least a basic understanding of taxonomy, the science and art of identification. Taxonomy is a very complicated, controversial, and highly personal science that many collectors just cannot grasp. But the rudiments of identification are necessary to any specialist collector and essential to collectors of some families, which is often another problem.

Specialized collecting is thus the most difficult type of collecting, but in my experience it can be the most personally satisfying. The sight of a large collection of cones or cowries or any other group displaying all the possible variations in size, color, pattern, and shape is simply fascinating.

Left: A selection of rare cones and cowries in a dealer's showcase. Photo by Dr. Herbert R. Axelrod at the Collector's Cabinet, New York. Right: Some common cowries and allied cowries. Top row (left to right): *Cypraea argus, Ovula ovum, Volva volva, C. tigris;* lower row: *C. vitellus, C. miliaris eburnea, C. erosa, C. carneola, C. isabella, C. limacina.* Photo by K. Gillett.

The Collection

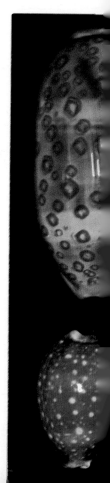

OBTAINING SHELLS

Shells themselves are found in almost all areas of the world, but relatively few of the over 100,000 snails and clams are of interest to most collectors. Even a casual look under leaves or litter in your back yard will reveal a few small land snails, but these little brown shells are of interest only to specialists in museums. Collectable shells can be obtained through informed self-collecting, through trades, by direct purchase in the foreign country of origin, and through purchase from dealers. All methods have their advantages and disadvantages.

Self-collecting is exactly that: collecting shells, either live or dead, yourself. Since virtually all collectable shells live in tropical

waters, the first prerequisite is the ability to travel to tropical shores. And by this I don't mean Florida, with its highly modified beaches crawling with tourists and already over-collected for the last fifty years. Some good collecting remains in Florida, but the areas are few and far between and the pickings very sparse. European shores are too cold. Western Africa is hard to reach, muddy, and has a limited but fascinating range of species; southern Africa is cold, but its beaches provide satisfactory dead specimens of many endemic (*i.e.*, found nowhere else) shells. Eastern Africa and most of the Indian Ocean countries are in political and economic turmoil and many favorite collecting areas are now unreachable. The Philippines is "wise" to the value of shells and difficult to move around in without contacts. Australia is gradually becoming over-collected and has a growing number of shelling restrictions, but some fascinating endemics make any trip worthwhile. The Pacific islands are either primitive enough to make obtaining specimens difficult or so touristy that the common shells for sale in native markets come from the Philippines and Florida. Japan is just so restrictive and expensive, as well as cool, that individual collecting is practically impossible. Many parts of the eastern Pacific coast are virtually inaccessible, but difficulties might be easily repaid with often rare and beautiful shells. The Caribbean still has many good shelling areas, but more and more near-shore collecting becomes difficult with the increasing number of tourists, and SCUBA is required to get worthwhile material. Although a few coastal states of the United States have collectable shells, most U.S. species are small and colorless, so little good material is to be found unless you are specifically interested in U.S. shells, which are much less collected than you might suppose.

Before attempting to go after more than a few beach shells in a foreign country (and many U.S. states), make sure you are not violating any local laws or customs. You certainly do not want to find yourself poaching in somebody's clam beds or want to get caught shelling without a permit that would have cost you just a token fee. This means that you should have contacts in a country before you can collect efficiently, as through a diving club, a shell club, a local dealer, or a tour arrangement that includes shelling provisions. If you plan on using SCUBA equipment, you will probably have to have copies of your certification or equivalent and may be surprised at the expense of renting equipment and the red tape required.

Beach collecting is the easiest type of self-collecting, but unfortunately it is also the least productive of worthwhile shells. By the time a dead shell is washed ashore it may have been at the mercy of the waves, grinding sand and gravel, and encrusting animals for months or perhaps even years. Even the rarest shells are worth little or nothing when in "bad beach" condition with areas of erosion, breaks, missing lips and spires, and faded colors. Most beach specimens are isolated valves of common intertidal clams and the eroded shells of small dull snails of various types found just at the low tide mark; neither are likely to be of interest to any but the extreme specialist (personally, I like little white clam shells, but not many people do). When you find the occasional beach cone or cowry, it is likely to be of a very common species and flawed in the bargain. Great finds do occur, of course, but they are few and far between. The best beach collecting is usually after heavy storms that have blown much debris—and shells—high onto the beach.

Collecting just below the tide marks with snorkel or glass-bottomed bucket can be much more profitable, and a good collection of at least locally common species can be made, often in very fresh or even live condition. Look especially near rocks or coral, but remember that currents in such areas may be dangerous to an outsider and the rocks may also harbor eels and sea urchins. Again, local contacts may be essential.

SCUBA is the most efficient way of collecting in most tropical areas, but it is of course expensive (especially rental of tanks, weight belts, and other equipment, as few people can afford to carry more than their own regulators around the world with them), time consuming (remember the red tape; also, there may be only one or two dive shops in an entire country, often many miles from that perfect reef you want to collect on), and dangerous (local information is a must when it comes to such things as the presence of sharks on certain reefs and seasonally dangerous water conditions).

Many collectors assume that once they get to the Philippines or Fiji they will run into the local store, buy a dredge and rent a

Cone shells are highly variable, both within a species and among the numerous species. Below are six specimens of *Conus purpurascens* taken from a single locality in the Galapagos Islands. Photo by the author. On the facing page are a few common Indo-Pacific cones. Top row (left to right): *Conus geographus, C. imperialis, C. striatus;* middle row: *C. aulicus, C. figulinus, C. miles, C. tulipa;* bottom row: *C. catus, C. suturatus, C. parvulus.* Photo by K. Gillett.

23

boat for a few dollars to get those rare deep-water species. First, there are probably precious few stores in the Philippines or Fiji (or Florida or Puerto Rico, for that matter) that ever heard of a dredge, let alone have one for sale. Few boats are suitable for using even the most simple type of dredge or trawl, as it requires a slow sustained speed for at least 15 or 30 minutes to have a chance of success. The fishing boats that may be acceptable will probably make more money by fishing than by rental, and the captain will probably want to stick to the grass flats and avoid the more varied and dangerous bottoms anyway. An outsider might also find himself in conflict with local fishermen or collectors. The same problems probably exist with any other scheme that revolves about purchasing local equipment.

The one advantage of self-collecting is that you collected the shells yourself. Years later you will be able to remember (perhaps with a bit of fantasy thrown in) just how you saw that conch partially buried in the sand or "rescued" that cowry from a vicious grouper. By the way, you might try to check the stomach contents of larger shell-eating fishes in local markets if you get the chance. Many groupers, snappers, and grunts, among others, "gulp" their food, including surprisingly rare shells. Several cowries were first known from such specimens (called *ex pisce)* and some are still collected most commonly from fishes.

Trading is a much simpler and less expensive, though almost as complicated, way of obtaining desired shells. First obtain a list of collectors in other countries and areas. I recommend the *International Directory of Conchologists* (The Shell Cabinet, P.O. Box 29, Falls Church, VA 22046) as the best I've seen so far. It and other directories are listings of collectors by state and country, usually with an indication of the group collected. Do not assume that just because a collector lives in, say, South Australia he or she will be able to get all South Australian shells, no more than you could get all the shells occurring in your section of the United States. If you are looking for something in particular, you will probably have to write a great many letters to many people.

To obtain something in trade, you must have something to trade. Although this sounds obvious, you will be amazed at how difficult it is to reach a good trade agreement with a potential trading partner. First, make sure you are speaking the same language—try to agree on a book or set of books to follow so you can be sure that any scientific names refer to the same species. Australian and Japanese books, for instance, commonly use not only different names for species, but different names for genera and families than do books written by authors in the U.S. or England. Once you make an agreement, stick to it, send your material promptly, and be sure it is packed to arrive in good condition. Did you remember to check with your trading partner on how to send the shells and who refunds postage, if anyone?

A few notes on shipping shells: the secret seems to lie in making sure that 1) the box isn't squashed flat, and 2) the shells don't move around within the box. Cotton, newspaper, and excelsior are all good and relatively cheap packing materials. Watch out for those little plastic boxes that look so nice and safe in your shell drawers—if a shell starts moving around in the box while in transit, it will end up looking like chicken mash by the time it travels a few thousand miles.

Some countries have import and export restrictions on shells, including fumigation requirements. Others will extract an import duty if any value is placed on the shells. The phrase "Specimen Seashells for Scientific Study—No Commercial Value" may not always be technically true, but it is very convenient. Registration of an expensive shell usually leads to expensive complications on the other end, including a visit to the Customs Office; are you sure the shell is so irreplaceable that it really *has* to be registered? Insured mail is sometimes even worse. Unregistered airmail or first class mail reaches its destination virtually all the time in most countries, but some countries do have a remarkably high loss rate, especially India, Sri Lanka, East African countries, and Indonesia. Trade at your own risk under such circumstances.

The shells you get through trading may not be the principal gain from the trade. You will also get to know interesting people in other countries and develop a correspondence that may last long after the last trade has been concluded.

Direct purchasing of shells in foreign countries is seldom a bargain. An amazing number of collectors even today believe that the natives of most African, Asian, and Pacific countries are still primitive and uninformed of shell values. They believe that

The intricate and colorful patterns of cones related to *Conus textile* are supposed to resemble woven cloth and tapestries, thus the name "textile cone" for any species with a similar pattern. Most textile cones are fish-eaters and have a venom dangerous to humans. Shown below is *Conus dalli,* an eastern Pacific textile cone prized by collectors. Photo by A. Kerstitch. Facing page: 1 & 2) Dorsal and ventral views of *Conus gloriamaris,* the glory-of-the-sea cone, a textile cone that was once the most widely known and perhaps most desirable of shells. 3 & 4) Dorsal and ventral views of *Conus hirasei,* a rare species with a very unusual color pattern; the periostracum is still present on the shell in photo 4. Photos by the author.

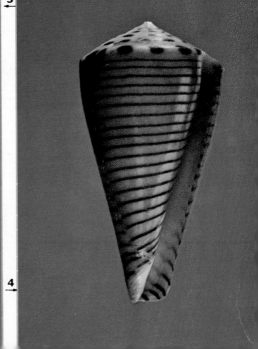

it is possible to go into the local market, find a local dealer with a few shells, and bargain him down to $10 or $20 for that $500 gem golden cowry. While this may have been true in the past (though I doubt it), it is not true today unless you are after obscure or difficult to identify little shells. Dealers in the Philippines, Tahiti, or Fiji, for instance, may have just as much recent literature on shells as you do, may get *Hawaiian Shell News*, often are members of a local dealers' organization, and sell shells for as much or even more than American dealers. With the currently fluctuating currencies, it is not uncommon to pay more for a shell in a Tahitian or Fijian market than for the same shell off an American dealer's list. Caution is strongly advised. Also, there are still a few (or is the number growing?) small foreign dealers that prey on the attitude of "superiority" of some foreign tourists. Be well informed about current identifications and values before you buy, and be sure to check that bargain rarity for repaired lips, holes filled with soap or wax, weights added to increase the adult "feel" of a subadult shell, or even spines glued onto that perfect murex with Elmer's glue. Foreign collectors and dealers are not gullible and are certainly not uninformed.

This leaves *dealers*. It is my opinion that the average collector—one who cannot afford the expense and time necessary for traveling—cannot exist without dealers and still obtain anything like a comprehensive collection. Dealers are the heart of shell collecting, just as dealers are essential to any other hobby. Some collectors consider dealers a necessary evil, and admittedly dealers do have their problems and flaws. If you are an "armchair collector" (one who doesn't do his own collecting) you may find it necessary to use dealers to obtain almost all your shells, and even an active self-collector often must go to dealers for that certain shell he just can't do without.

Dealers fall into two basic categories that sometimes overlap: dealers through shops and dealers through the mails. Shell shops dealing in commercial shells are relatively common and can be found in any large city and any resort area. These handle the larger or more attractive shells, butterflies, insects embedded in plastic, etc., as well as shell curios. A few handle specimen-quality shells, but usually in very limited numbers and variety. An established shop usually has a large overhead, such as rent, utilities, clerks, even local advertising, and depends on large numbers of people passing through each business day. Thus their prices tend to be on the high side of market value and you might have to fight your way through the purple sea urchin lamps, souvenir engraved queen conchs, giant clam valves, and mineral displays to find the specimen shells. By carefully checking shells in such a store you can often make good purchases at decent prices. Unless the store has a resident manager who knows his shells, don't expect much help from the clerks—they often know as little about shells as they do about what makes the cash register work. By all means check shell shops whenever you run into them—you never know what you might find.

Recently pet shops have realized that there is a natural tie-in between marine aquarium enthusiasts and shell enthusiasts. It is becoming more and more common to see at least a few common shells being sold in pet shops that handle marine fishes. Not only can this combination make shells available to people living in towns that are too small to support shell shops, but it also helps promote the hobby by bringing shells to the attention of people who otherwise might never become aware of their beauty and interest.

Mail-order shell dealers are numerous and varied. The last few years have seen an increasing number of small dealers equivalent to the "vest pocket" dealers of stamp collecting fame. These are usually individuals with limited stocks of a very few species (often no more than 50 or 100, mostly cones, cowries, and murexes) who put out mimeographed lists once a year or so. The specimens are usually obtained from wholesalers in the Philippines, Red Sea area, and Tahiti, so one dealer's list looks much like any other's. The shells are often reasonably priced, and occasionally a real bargain can be found. The main disadvantages of dealing with such small dealers are lack of abundant material and lack of a history in the business so their reliability can be judged. However, some small dealers are actually collectors recently returned from months or years in exotic locales, so it is sometimes possible to find small dealers with shells from very unusual places.

Numerous larger and well-established shell dealers are found in the United States, Europe, and several other foreign countries.

Two cold-water Japanese volutes, *Fulgoraria prevostiana* (1) and *Fulgoraria hirasei* (2). Compare these drab shells with the Australian volutes on the facing page. From *Shells of Japan* by T. Okutani, Kodansha Publishers.

A selection of colorful volutes from Australian waters. Top row (left to right): *Volutoconus grossi, Cymbiolacca complexa, Cymbiolacca wisemani;* bottom row: *Amoria maculata, Cymbiola sophiae, Cymbiolacca pulchra.* Most dealers list all volutes under the single genus *Voluta* for convenience. Photo by K. Gillett.

Such dealers put out more frequent lists (often every six or eight weeks) that are printed and feature a larger variety of material, often including moderately rare or very rare specimens. Usually price lists are free to regular customers, but due to increasing costs, more and more dealers are asking from $1 to $3 for subscriptions to their lists.

A good price list presents the shells alphabetically by scientific name, often by subspecies and varieties as well as species (and sometimes grouped by family). Usually there is at least an indication of the country of origin. Size will be indicated in either metric or English units, often as a range such as 14-22mm (usually the first orders for a shell get the larger and nicer specimens), and there will be either abbreviations for condition (to be explained later) or a verbal description of condition. Prices vary considerably from dealer to dealer and from list to list in some cases, even for material that came from the same overseas suppliers. Because a mail-order business has a relatively lower overhead than a shop, prices are commonly lower, especially for medium-priced shells. Few shells sell for less than 50^{c} today, at least in the major families, and most retail in the $2 to $10 range, with many cheaper and many more expensive on any average list.

As mentioned, there are good and bad points to buying from dealers. First, it gives the collector access to almost unlimited material in not only the major families but also many smaller and less popular families. Second, it is convenient to just go over a list and write up an order or phone it in; in a few weeks, you have your shells. No matter how often you've done it, it is still thrilling to open a box of new shells. Third, by comparing prices and conditions on various lists, it is possible to obtain a good proportion of your shells at very reasonable prices, certainly less than the cost of collecting them yourself.

All the disadvantages rest on understanding and trusting your dealer. You do not really *know* what shell you will get until you see it, for several worthless names are still common on price lists of all dealers. It is common to find what is certainly the same shell listed under two or three different names at different prices on one list. To order successfully from a price list you simply must know your shells, or you will have some very rude surprises awaiting you. Such identification problems are seldom actually the fault of dealers, but just due to the confusion present in identification of shells. A few dealers, however, do take advantage of many collectors' tendencies to purchase "new names" without checking to see if these are actually representative of new shells as well. Experience—and perhaps a few wasted dollars—will teach you which dealers do this. Fortunately, good dealers feature a return privilege, so you may be inconvenienced but seldom cheated.

You must also learn from experience just how a dealer grades his shells. Most say they follow the HMS-ISGS system explained later, but shell grading is a very subjective art and some dealers tend to grade high or low on certain types of shells. This is sometimes part of the reason for price differences among different lists.

There is also the question of whether you can or cannot trust the locality data that comes with a shell. Wholesalers supply data with the shells they sell to dealers; dealers then recopy the data on the label of the shell you buy. Some errors can of course occur in such recopying, but this is not the major problem. It is a simple fact that detailed locality data on shells coming from foreign countries, especially the Philippines, is often or usually wrong. This has to be accepted unless you confine yourself to shells collected by personal friends you can trust—which would lead to very small collections for most collectors. Take the information on the label, compare it carefully with the shell and literature on variation in the species, and make up your own mind as to whether or not to trust it. Frankly, for most purposes country is about as good information as you can get, although with Australia it helps to know if the shell came from the eastern coast or western coast. Shells coming through Taiwan are best treated as being without locality data. It seems that shells from Taiwanese trawlers across the Indo-Pacific must be jumbled together with no effort to keep track of individual data. By knowing the species you can tell pretty certainly which species come from Australia or Hawaii, but there have been numerous Indian Ocean shells sold as from the "China Sea." The same thing happens with dredged material from Japanese suppliers—numerous mix-ups of Japanese and Hawaiian species have occur-

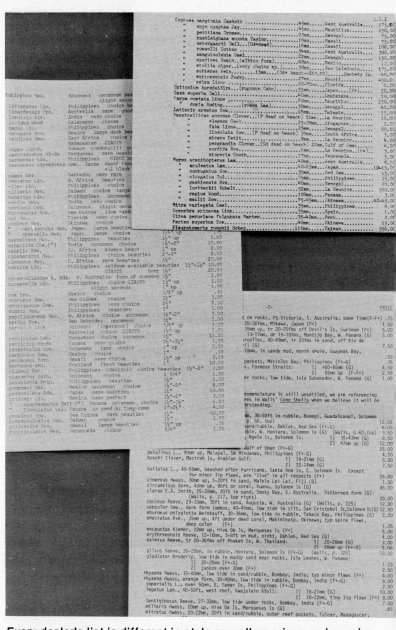

Every dealer's list is different in style as well as prices and species offered. These three typical lists exhibit differences in grading notation, metric and English measurement, and locality indication, for instance. Photo by Glen S. Axelrod.

The last steps in cleaning a cone shell. 1) Clorox, a toothbrush, forceps, and a small container are used to dissolve the periostracum and animal fragments, after which a light coating of baby oil restores the sheen. 2) Careful brushing helps remove adherent periostracum. 3) A comparison of an almost clean *Conus virgo* (right) with its uncleaned counterpart (left). Photos by Glen S. Axelrod.

2

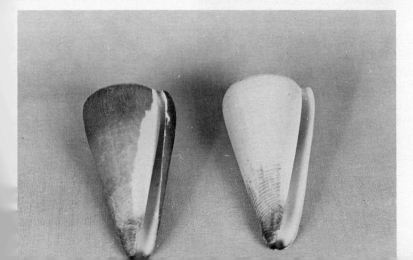

red, especially with rarer deep-water shells taken in coral dredges. So take all labels with a grain of salt. By the way, even museum specimens commonly have incorrect data, so the problem is not restricted to dealer-purchased shells.

In dealings with at least fifty different dealers, large and small, American and foreign, I have only been cheated once, and even that may have been due to a misunderstanding. I have gotten satisfactory service from all other dealers, although sometimes the word "satisfactory" might be a slight exaggeration of the facts. I currently deal regularly with at least four dealers that I've used for several years. Each has his own peculiarities, good points, and bad points, but from experience it is possible to weigh each list and seldom be disappointed with the shells ordered. Phone calls help, too, and sometimes with more expensive shells it is worth the few dollars for a call to get more information.

Foreign dealers vary from very good and trustworthy to crooked. Be cautious of any dealer with large numbers of "new" species on his list at very high prices. Be cautious of any dealer that demands payment by bank check or money order *before* the shells are sent. Always keep your first order small until you get to know the dealer. Be cautious of any dealer that demands minimum orders of $50 or more unless you have the money to spare just in case something goes wrong, or unless you can get together with friends to make up the order at minimum individual risk. The moment you get one "doctored" (altered) shell from a dealer, drop him like a hot brick—at least that is my opinion. If you notice one doctored shell, you probably have more in your collection already from the same dealer. If you are cautious, you can get very good deals from foreign dealers, as they are often wholesalers. Remember, though, that foreign shipments may take three to six months to reach you by sea mail, that foreign postage is expensive, and that there are often complications in making payments to foreign countries. Also be careful with scientific names used on foreign lists—they are often obviously incorrect.

Two other types of dealers deserve brief mention. The first type is the dealer that sells mostly rare material ("one-of-a-kind") on a first-come, first-serve basis. Several such dealers advertise regularly in shell publications, but I've had limited dealings with them. Frankly, the material they sell is either available from my regular dealers or so expensive that it's beyond my budget anyway. They also tend to have what might be called rather "exclusive clientele" and often don't answer letters of enquiry from strangers. I suppose they are just as reliable as any other dealers, but it seems the temptations of higher priced shells might lead to some rather shady operators creeping in occasionally. The last dealer type is the private collector selling his collection through a handwritten or xeroxed list sent through the mails. Frankly, I have yet to see anything on such a list that I would trust purchasing. Often the shells are obviously misnamed, over-priced, without any indications of data or condition, and just not worth taking the risk. There are collectors, however, who will take any risk rather than purchase from a "real" dealer—I suppose these sale lists are aimed at such collectors, who must have more stubbornness than brains in some cases.

CONDITION AND GRADING

If an army travels on its stomach, then a shell travels on its condition. A specimen of the rarest species is almost worthless if its condition is extremely poor, and even a specimen of a common species often fetches a nice price when the condition is truly excellent. But the problem is how to grade a shell's condition in such a manner that a collector knows what to expect from a few letters on a dealer's list. Several methods have been used, from general descriptions such as "really nice," "gorgeous," or "bad beach" to the rather complicated and often hard to apply HMS-ISGS (Hawaiian Malacological Society—International Shell Grading System). The most practical answer is probably somewhere between these extremes.

The HMS-ISGS has been revised in part a few times since its original introduction, but its basic form consists of the following condition grades:

Gem (G): a perfect specimen, with an unblemished spire, unbroken spines, and lips without chips, fully adult and normally colored; a shell without a flaw, well cleaned both inside and out;

cowries must have original color and gloss; bivalves must have both valves, properly matched and unbroken.

Fine (F): an adult shell with only minor flaws and with not more than one shallow growth mark; must have original color and gloss; a cone may have a rough lip or one small chip, and the spire must be unblemished; a murex may have not more than two minor frond breaks; no repairs—filed lips or mended knobs, for example—permitted. [A filed lip is one that has been filed or ground down on an emery stone to hide chips and breaks; cones are very often filed.]

Good (Gd): a reasonably acceptable shell with a few defects such as growth marks, broken spines, worn spire, or lip chips; minor fading of color permitted; specimen may be slightly subadult; a good quality shell that must faithfully display all the basic characters of the species.

Fair (Fr): may be obviously dead or beach collected with chipped lips, faded color, growth faults or imperfect spires; this grade is about equivalent to an average commercial shell.

Another and more simple system was proposed by the Morrison Galleries and is somewhat more practical and flexible:

Gem: a mature shell with no noticeable flaws.

Fine: a minor flaw or flaws that do not detract significantly from appearance; shell may be slightly subadult.

Good: a noticeable flaw or flaws, or some wear or fading.

Fair: a shell with significant damage and/or substantial wear.

Plus and minus signs are used with both systems to indicate conditions slightly better or worse than the stated grade. Additionally, with either system you must rely on the dealer to state any oddities of condition, whether good or bad, such as worm holes, abraded areas, or exceptional color. Beach shells must be stated as such. Almost all dealers indicate if an operculum (perc) is present with the shell, but it is best to ignore this part of the description as opercula are often mismatched to the shell and may even come from a different species. Sometimes I think that some foreign dealers just have bins labeled "percs" and send out one at random with any shell sold. Also, in most shells it is practically impossible to tell a freshly dead shell from one taken alive, so don't pay extra for the perc that "proves" the shell was live-taken—it isn't necessarily so.

CLEANING AND STORAGE

Since shells are part of living animals, it stands to reason that at some time or other the remains of the animal must be removed unless you wish your collection to have a "ripe" smell on humid days. There are many ways of *cleaning* a shell, and each collector who self-collects probably has a favorite method. The simplest way is to leave the shell, with animal intact or the larger part of the foot removed, in a shady place in or under the sand and let the flies and other insects gradually eat the flesh. When decomposition has proceeded sufficiently (a few days to a few weeks), the shell is repeatedly rinsed with cold water and any remaining chunks of flesh are removed with a bent wire or knitting needle. Of course this method takes time and the smell may get rather strong, but it is simple. When rinsing the shell, be sure to keep the operculum with the specimen it came from. Cowries may be dulled by burial in sand.

With some shells it is possible to simply kill the animal by drowning it in water that has been heated (to remove the air) and then cooled, and then pulling out the flesh with forceps or a wire using a rotating motion. Rinsing follows. This is probably the safest method with polished species.

Freezing also is efficient if the facilities are available. Place the carefully padded shell with animal in the freezer for a day or two, then completely thaw it out for a day. Refreeze and then thaw again. This results in decomposition of the large muscles of the animal, which can be rapidly removed and the shell rinsed. (Cowries and other nacreous shells may develop fine cracks from too much heat or cold.)

As shells are composed of calcium, they react to acids, no matter how mild. If you don't believe this, just drop a garbage shell into vinegar, a very weak solution of acetic acid (one of the weaker acids), and watch the bubbles indicating chemical activity. An acid-treated shell appears dull and lusterless. Decomposition of flesh results in the formation of weak acids that can etch a polished shell and destroy the gloss. This is especially dangerous with cowries, which can be severely damaged by just leaving them in water overnight or by letting the decomposing flesh touch the base of the shell during cleaning. So don't store uncleaned shells in water, and always try to keep them with the aperture or mouth up so the acids do not ooze out and touch the outside of the shell.

Shells with animals can be preserved in 40% to 70% ethyl or isopropyl alcohol, but there is always a risk of discoloration from contaminants in the alcohol. This method results in not only efficient temporary storage of shells, but also in preservation of the animal for studies of its anatomy if desired. Small snails are commonly preserved, then dried intact. Once preserved, however, it is often virtually impossible to completely remove the animal from the shell. Formalin, an acid, must never be used near shells as even the vapor can damage the shell's surface.

Shells with a periostracum (brownish or colorless, often hairy, external covering) often or usually must be cleaned of the covering before they can be completely identified. Cowries and olives do not have a periostracum, but in cones it often is thick and ugly. The periostracum may be removed by soaking the shell in a 50% solution of household Clorox® liquid, then brushing with an old toothbrush. To be safe, don't leave the shell in longer than necessary, though the Clorox® won't hurt a normal shell even during a prolonged soaking. Delicately colored mouths may be protected by a thin layer of petroleum jelly if desired, though this is usually unnecessary. (Clorox® makes the finger-tips slippery, so be careful when handling the shell.) Some collectors like to keep shells in pairs of one cleaned and one with the periostracum intact and preserved by soaking in alcohol and glycerine. I like to coat the entire cleaned shell with a *small* amount of mineral oil to return the natural gloss, but some collectors feel this is an "unnatural" act. Personally, I think shells without periostracum and treated with oil are more attractive and easier to identify than those left in a "natural" state. Opercula are usually glued (use a water-soluble glue) to a small piece of cotton and placed in the mouth of the shell.

If you have accurate data with the shell, be sure to keep it with the specimen at all times during the cleaning operation. Most papers (including index cards) dissolve in water and alcohol, by the way, but the heavy paper of tie-on style shipping tags holds up well and is readily available; write with a soft pencil. Many label formats for use with cleaned shells are available, some in pads from dealers, but any slip of paper that gives locality, date, and any other information on the shell will do. Museums usually assign catalog numbers to specimens and then ink these numbers on the shells, but private collections could easily be ruined by such a method. First, the market for inked shells is considerably reduced, and second, inked numbers often partially rub off. I find that the label when folded will fit into the mouth of most shells and wedge there firmly enough to ensure that it will not be lost or switched. When several specimens are from one locality (a suite or lot) and kept in a single tray, most collectors use a single tray label—inside the tray, not outside. Of course if you drop two or more trays of shells you have a problem, but careful handling will hopefully avert that problem.

Storing your shells is perhaps the most thorny problem you will face. Under no circumstances should shells be exposed to light, especially sunlight. They fade—the fading may be slow, but sooner or later they all go. So any type of coffee table or bookcase display is out, and for that matter so is any continual display. Shells should be stored so they are relatively cool, not in high humidity, and in the dark.

The best method of housing is a cabinet with numerous large, shallow drawers—a shell cabinet. These are expensive, hard to obtain today, and take up a lot of space in an apartment or modern small house. A good dealer may be able to direct you to someone who still makes shell cabinets, or you might on rare occasions be able to get a used one from a museum—but don't hold your breath. More readily available, but in the $300 to $500 or more range, is a cabinet designed to store insect boxes, the boxes themselves serving as drawers. The entomology department of any college should be able to put you in touch with a company that sells such cabinets. Most hold about twenty or twenty-four drawers about 18″ × 18″, so they hold a lot of shells.

Within the drawers you need trays. These can be cut from a good grade of posterboard and held together with strong tape. They needn't be fancy, just effective. Using sizes in even multiples makes most efficient use of room in the drawer and gives you a proper size tray for almost any shell or combination of shells. The trays I use with good success are 1½ × 1 × 1″, 3 × 1 × 1″, 3 × 2 × 1″, and 6 × 3 × 1″, but you may need different sizes for the shells you collect. You seldom need trays

1

2

Methods of housing shells if space and money are no problems. Opposite: 1) A typical shell cabinet with 10 drawers designed to hold shells of different sizes. 2) An end table with a few small drawers and a glass-topped section to exhibit shells. Below: 3) The shell room of an advanced collector—and every collector's dream. These photos were taken by Leslie Easland, Orlando, Florida, accomplished designer and craftsman of high quality shell cabinets.

3

Trays of many types are suitable for holding shells. Shown here are a plastic box (top left) with protruding hinges and clasp, a small jewelry box sitting in its own lid (next to plastic box in top row), and four sizes of home-made posterboard trays. Also shown are a couple of glass vials used for small specimens. Photo by Glen S. Axelrod.

more than 1″ deep except for large or oddly shaped shells. Very small shells are kept in glass vials, while larger shells are simply placed in the trays with their labels. A thin layer of cotton or color-fast foam should line the trays to help cushion the shells; strips of cotton can also be placed between and alongside the shells for extra safety.

Plastic boxes are used by many collectors and look very nice, but I personally don't like them. They are very expensive, the hinges and clasp (if present) take up a lot of room, and they don't come in convenient sizes to fill a drawer properly.

If a cabinet is too expensive for you, a sturdy chest of drawers with the shallowest drawers you can find (2″ to 4″ is best) is quite acceptable and will hold quite a few shells.

With the trend toward smaller living quarters, often a cabinet just won't fit even if you can find one. If you are collecting mostly small or medium shells, try the metal boxes with plastic trays used to hold small parts. These are available in most hardware or department stores, are relatively cheap, come in a variety of sizes, and with extra partitions will hold many shells. In some ways they are more convenient than cabinets as no cardboard trays are required and the shells fit snugly into their spaces. The fronts of the transparent plastic drawers should be covered with paper to keep out the light. One problem: if the cabinet is jarred or turned over, small shells may "drift" over the tops of the trays into other compartments. Most cabinets come with hanging holes and can be mounted on a wall or on pegboard. A combination of these small parts cabinets and a chest of drawers for larger shells is cheap and works well in limited space.

The preceding notes on cleaning and storage are obviously very general and should always be taken with a grain of salt. Some shells just do not clean well, while others, such as cowries and murexes, are very delicate during cleaning and easily damaged. I've yet to understand how anyone stores a collection of large shells in a small apartment or manages to safely store murexes and other spiny specimens, but obviously many people do.

One last note on collections as such. If you get tired of a part of your collection and cannot find a market, don't throw it away. If there is good data with the shells any museum will be glad to take your collection, and there may even be an income tax credit involved. Even if your collection is the dregs, museums usually find some convenient way of disposing of the leftovers.

Left: *Tellina radiata.* Some tellins are attractively colored, so the family is considered marginally collectable. Photo by G. Marcuse. Right: Variation in *Conus mercator.* A series such as this is the goal of many specialized cone collectors. Photo by P. Carmichael.

Now
The
Shells

The diversity of the Mollusca, the phylum or major animal group to which belong the snails, clams, squids, etc., is almost incredible at first glance. To think that the headless bivalved clams belong to the same group as the intelligent eight-armed octopuses is difficult at first, but undoubtedly so. No one really knows just how many species of molluscs exist, but there are estimates of between 100,000 and 200,000 species; some say there are over 100,000 species of just snails. We are interested here only in those groups that are collectable—the shells many people collect and are willing to spend money for.

Although collecting trends vary from time to time, at the moment collectable shells can be broken into about six groups by

popularity. We'll briefly mention some of the popular shells of each group, but obviously the shell kingdom is just too large to even attempt to summarize it in a few pages. So what follows is only a brief overview and certainly not comprehensive. There are many books on the shells themselves that we'll look at in the next chapter.

THE BIG ONES

Four families of snails dominate all others in their popularity. All are at least moderately attractive shells, each family with its share of beautiful species and its share of colorless "dogs," but each family contains over 100 species, many of which are rare and expensive. The general collector is likely to get no more than 50 or so species of each family, and even the advanced specialist collector is unlikely to complete any family. Cones and cowries are undoubtedly the most popular shells, although no one really knows for sure which is the most popular of the two. Closely following them are the volutes, generally expensive and rather exclusive shells. Recently the murexes have moved from the second-most-popular list into the big time with the publication of more literature and discovery of new species.

Cones

This complex family (Conidae) of over 300 species and numerous subspecies and varieties is my personal favorite. The species vary from slender brown shells to extremely thick and rather globular species with solid white or black and white patterns. Some are glossy, others knobby; some are brightly colored in reds and blues, but admittedly most are not very colorful. Cones have the reputation of being hard to identify, a direct consequence of their often extreme variability. Probably the greatest attraction of collecting cones is that there is always another variety to obtain, even if you already have most of the species in your price range.

Included in this family are some of the great rarities of shell collecting, such as *Conus cervus*, *Conus milneedwardsi*, and *Conus dusaveli*. The glory-of-the-seas cone, *Conus gloriamaris*, is probably one of the best known species to non-collectors as it has been widely publicized for its rarity and many legends have grown up around it. Now, however, it is collected frequently in the Philippines, Solomons, and New Guinea, and its value has decreased from $1,000 or $1,500 to about $300 to $600, still respectable but no great rarity.

With only a dozen or so exceptions, cones are all tropical species mostly found on shallow reefs or sand flats. A couple of dozen species are found only in deep water and are virtually never seen alive. In fact, many cones are seldom found in truly gem condition.

Cowries

Ranking with cones as the most popular family, the cowries (Cypraeidae) are a smaller family of fewer than 200 species. Few of the species are large, with many well under an inch in length. All have the attraction of smooth, polished shells with a narrow toothed mouth. Their gloss and often beautiful colors and patterns have long made them favorites with collectors, and they are likely to stay at or near the most popular family level forever.

Deserving separate mention is the golden cowry, *Cypraea aurantium*, a four-inch bright golden orange shell once used on the necklaces of tribal chiefs on Pacific islands. Now they are taken regularly in many localities, but their price continues to rise because of their popularity and demand—$350 to $450 is now normal for a nice shell (few truly gem golden cowries exist). Numerous very rare cowries are avidly sought after, including *Cypraea valentia, Cypraea fultoni, Cypraea broderipii*, and *Cypraea leucodon*. Many collectors specialize in the odd cowries of Australian waters, the larger species of the subgenus *Zoila* and the small *Notocypraea*. Several toothless or dorsally ridged species are endemic to cool waters of South Africa and are virtually never taken alive, with even worn beach shells being quite acceptable to collectors.

I should also mention here the shells called "cowry allies" as they are often collected by cowry specialists as well. These include trivias (very small, often dorsally ridged shells that look like dull miniature cowries), eratos (very small jug-shape shells often confused with marginellas), and the ovulids. Ovulids are a varied group of often spindle-shaped or cylindrical shells tending toward white or apricot in color and seldom with distinct patterns. Many are small (under half an inch), but the larger species are attractive and interesting. The flamingo tongues *(Cyphoma)*

49

are glossy shells of a peach color, toothless mouth, and often a heavy dorsal ridge; they are common Caribbean shells living on sea whips and sea fans. Unfortunately, the ovulids are taxonomically difficult shells and presently greatly over-priced for their size and interest, which limits their importance to collectors.

Volutes

These are often very large and cumbersome shells that have been called the "aristocrats" of the shell world, probably because there are so few common species in the family. Of the about 200 species, only a couple of dozen, if that many, can be purchased for under $5, and most of the species are in the $20 to $60 range, with several major rarities. Volutes are more typical of cooler waters than the other major families, with many of the species coming from Australia. Some are nicely formed, rather elongated shells with simple spotted or striped patterns, while others are dull brown shapeless shells that even a mother would find difficult to love. The animals of many species are much more attractive than the shells.

Murexes

Spiny shells never appeal to me, but apparently many collectors are beginning to appreciate the "delicate beauty" of the murexes (more properly called muricids), family Muricidae. These are usually whitish shells of about an inch to six inches in length, sometimes more, with well developed spines and fronds (plate-like "wings" or frills). Many species are indeed truly graceful shells, but they are again a group with few characters, making identifications difficult. Although many species are common and inexpensive, the group has its share of expensive shells and true rarities, including quite a few supposedly new species described each year. Murexes are growing in popularity faster than any other family, except perhaps the miters.

"Murex allies" include several families or subfamilies of murex-like shells that may not be closely related to the true Muricidae. These include the latiaxids, small deep-water shells with often extensively developed frills and odd shell shapes; the thaids, usually plain shells related to the common oyster drills; and the typhids, delicate, small deep-water shells of often rather bizarre but graceful shapes. Latiaxids and typhids are usually expensive shells, some of them extremely hard to obtain.

SECOND STRING

This group is even harder to define than the big four, but it consists basically of the next most popular families. I only include here four families, although many collectors would vote to include some of the "also rans" here.

Conchs, family Strombidae, are a relatively small family (about 75 species) but include many familiar species. The larger species such as the queen conch *(Strombus gigas)* and the spider conchs *(Lambis)* are familiar in curio shops around the world. Of the main families we will mention, this and the pectens are the only ones that commonly provide food for human consumption wherever they are found, with conch chowder being a familiar bill of fare in the Caribbean. Several small species are abundant enough to be used in jewelry. This is one of the few (or perhaps the only) major families that can be completed on a limited budget, with no species currently selling for more than $300. Most species are in the $1 to $5 range, and there are many varieties and subspecies to keep a collector busy while trying to get the difficult species. The larger shells tend to be heavy and knobby, thus difficult to store, but their brownish or creamy shells do not fade readily, which leads to them being just placed on bookcases or used as door stops (horror of horrors!).

The elongated, highly polished shells of the *olives,* family Olividae, are familiar to collectors and non-collectors alike as they are often used in jewelry. Most collectors stick with the confusing species and varieties of the genus *Oliva,* which according to different interpretations has from twenty to seventy-five or more species. The shells have much the same attractions as cowries, but suffer from badly confused taxonomy and an over-emphasis in the past on very minor and intergrading varieties. *Oliva porphyria* is a large (four inches) netted-pattern species of great popularity; in the past it is said that excited collectors have confused this with *Conus gloriamaris,* but I suspect this is just one more unfounded shell legend. Black olives occur as individual varieties in several species, as do white olives, brown olives, and reddish olives; all have unfortunately been given separate names. Olives inhabit shallow sandy flats in most cases and can be collected by attracting them to rotting fish or following their trails in the sand.

The "olive allies" also belong to the Olividae and include the ancillids and olivellids. Neither group is as popular as the true olives, but this will probably change if and when ancillids reach the market in larger numbers. Ancillids are usually deep-water shells of small to quite large size and usually some shade of brown, often with lighter bands at the shoulder. The spire is commonly nacred-over or callused so the individual whorls are no longer visible. There is no popular literature on this group of nearly 100 species, some of which are very rare and fascinating shells deserving more attention. Olivellids, mostly *Olivella*, look like miniature olives, many species being under half an inch in length. Their small size discourages collectors, as does a lack of literature on identification.

The families Cymatiidae and Bursidae, *tritons* or *frog shells*, are treated as a unit because the shells somewhat resemble each other and are not that carefully distinguished by collectors. Cymatiidae includes such genera as *Distorsio*, which are oddly twisted shells with strong teeth on the lips; *Apollon* or *Biplex*, with some species greatly flattened and with beautiful fronds; *Cymatium*, rather knobby and cumbersome shells of an interesting diversity; and *Charonia*, the Triton's trumpet shells once actually used to make primitive horns. Bursidae look much like cymatiids but have a distinct notch or canal for the posterior siphon at the back edge of the mouth. The major genus is *Bursa*, moderately large shells with often brightly colored mouths but otherwise not that interesting in appearance. Misidentifications are rampant in this group, but many species are readily available at moderate prices, while others are very difficult to obtain but not excessively expensive once you find them.

ALSO RANS

Included here are basically the rest of the larger, collectable marine snails, as almost every family has its adherents. Some of the families are quite to moderately popular with collectors and include interesting and attractive shells, while others are too small, too plain, or too rare to be of more than peripheral interest. Usually about a third to half of a dealer's list will be of species in these miscellaneous families, but some, such as the miters, are gaining in popularity each year as more material and literature become available.

Miters, family Mitridae, are usually small, pointed shells with brownish patterns, but one group (probably a full family), the vexillums, are often strikingly patterned with bands of red, yellow, or white on brown. Most species sell in the 50$^{\epsilon}$ to $2 price range, but some of the larger and more attractive species may fetch $10 to $50 and occasionally more. Dealers seem to currently be increasing the number of species sold, so I suspect the miters will be a "second string" family shortly.

Marginellas (Marginellidae) are attractive and somewhat cowry-like glossy shells, but they suffer from the disadvantage that a great many of the species in the family Marginellidae are very small (quarter of an inch to half an inch) and whitish, with identifications virtually impossible. Some larger (about two inches) and attractively patterned species are found in western and southern Africa, however, and are the center of popularity in the family. One large species, the South African *Afrivoluta pringlei,* was originally thought to be a volute until the animal was studied; once rare, it is now only moderately expensive.

Cassids, family Cassidae, include usually thick, toothed-mouth shells often called the helmet shells. Included are several moderately small and attractive shells, but many of the species are large, cumbersome, heavily eroded when adult, and simply not very attractive. Few collectors collect the entire family but instead pick and choose the more attractive and interesting species of the family. Cameos were originally carved in a Mediterranean species of the family. *Tun shells* (Tonnidae) and *fig shells* (Ficidae) are vaguely similar to helmets but thinner and less complicated shells. There are only a few species in each family, but their identification is presently almost impossible.

Terebrids (Terebridae) are greatly elongated, very slender shells that appear to be mostly spire. Most of the species are large enough to be enjoyable (an inch or so) and many are very attractively patterned. The family is fairly large, over 200 species, and several dozen species can be purchased with relative ease; few species are expensive. *Harps* (Harpidae) are largely body whorl, with little spire, and are covered with sharp ribs; the few species range in price from 50¢ to over $600, so this is a difficult family to complete.

Wentletraps (Epitoniidae) look vaguely like terebrids but are covered with strong or weak narrow ribs that give the shells a distinctive appearance. Most species are small (under an inch) and white, but they are popular with quite a few collectors. Many of the species are quite expensive for their size. Naticids or *moon snails* (Naticidae) are attractive shells related to cowries and having many species with a nice gloss and pattern. Most species, however, are rather plain and few are carried by dealers. The same is true of *nerites* (Neritidae), primitive snails best known for their often attractively colored mouths, odd opercula, and abundance in shallow waters around the world; few species are of interest to collectors, although two or three species with long spines always find a ready market.

Abalones (Haliotidae) are more familiar to collectors and gourmets on the West Coast of the United States. These are small to quite large (half an inch to over eight inches), virtually untwisted snails that live like limpets attached to the bottom; there is a series of holes running along the margin of the shell. The interior of the shell is a brilliant mother-of-pearl, so the shells are often used for ash trays. The about 60 species are sometimes brightly colored and very interesting, with a few rarities and several species very difficult to obtain. Others are the by-products of commercial fisheries for the edible foot (abalone steak) in California and Australia, so the condition of such species is very poor, with heavy encrustations and worm holes. *Limpets* themselves are a group of several families characterized by the simple, flattened or conical shells. They are very difficult to identify, usually in poor condition because of the rough waters they often inhabit, and seldom attractive, but the very large species of South Africa, Japan, Australia, and the East Pacific are not unpopular.

Top shells and *turbans* include a great number of species of two very similar families, Trochidae and Turbinidae, distinguished by the operculum. Species with unusual shapes, attractive patterns, or spines usually are sold by dealers under a variety of names, often incorrect, but the group is at best marginal in collector interest. An exception is the large genus *Calliostoma,* often brilliantly colored glossy shells of delicate sculpture; they are usually deep-water shells and include several rare species that seldom fetch what they are really worth. *Angaria* and *Astraea* are called star shells because of the projections at the edges of the whorls. *Turbo,* a large genus of coarse shells used to produce mother-of-pearl buttons, is more noted for the glossy green operculum called a cat's eye.

Finally, I can't leave the miscellaneous shells without mentioning slit shells, family Pleurotomariidae. Although the family possesses fewer than 25 living species, they are the most exclusive of the snails, with no species selling for under $200 when in excellent condition and most species selling in the $400 to $800 range; one species has sold for as much as $5,000. Even a moderately nice specimen of the most common Japanese species seldom fails to attract attention.

TWO FOR ONE

Pectens, clams, oysters, coquinas, and dozens of other types of shells constitute the bivalves. These shells are exactly that—bivalved, with two valves or shells. The shells are held together in life by strong muscles and usually small projections called "teeth" on the "hinge" where the shells join. The teeth have a complicated and very confused terminology with dozens of terms applied to various conditions of their development, but these are seldom used in collector literature—perhaps fortunately. Although bivalves are common from the tide line to the deep sea and from pole to pole, they are not very popular with collectors. Few bivalves have brilliant colors, many are fragile, most are larger than collectable snails, and they are difficult to store because you have to keep the valves together somehow (many people wrap them with string or rubber bands, but since many species are oval it's hard to make this hold; a drop of Elmer's glue on the hinge works, but the shell must then be soaked in water if you have to see the inside). Except for the pectens, which have regained a long-deserved popularity, bivalves sold by dealers are a mixed lot of just about anything they can obtain, as there appear to be few groups that are really considered collectable. We'll thus cover pectens first, then "the rest."

The term pecten is applied in a broad sense to what most people call scallops plus such things as spiny oysters *(Spondylus)* and limas. True pectens are the family Pectinidae, spiny oysters Spondylidae, and limas Limidae. There are numerous genera in the Pectinidae, ranging from translucent minute deep-water types to thickened, attached, distorted rock-dwellers, but dealers generally sell them all as *Pecten*. Sometimes they use *Chlamys* for species with unequal "ears" (projections on either side of the hinge area) and *Amusium* for very smooth species, but it is doubtful if either of these generic names has any real relation to the actual genera, which are poorly defined. There are anywhere from 250 to 450 living pectens, but virtually no literature on how to identify them.

In the course of a year, it is normal to see about 100 to 150 species of pectens (in the broad sense) offered for sale, these ranging in price from 50ᶜ to $75 or more, with most in the $1 to $5 range. The species come from all seas, including cold polar waters, and all continents (even a few from the subantarctic islands of New Zealand). Many pectens are delicate shades of pink or yellow, with a considerable number of species violet to purple or red. Many species are heavily ribbed, while a few have erect thorn-like spines or fluid-filled nodules on the ribs. *Spondylus* are larger shells, often red or solid white in color, and with large pointed or flattened spines in most species. Limas are usually small and delicate, smooth or finely spined, and white or brownish, but some species reach over four inches in length and are bright yellow.

Pectens hold the same natural fascination for some people as do cones or cowries, and it is certain that with adequate literature at the collector level this would rapidly become one of the top four or five of the major families.

Although they are not really related to pectens, the chamas (Chamidae) or jewel boxes have a vague resemblance to *Spondylus* and rank with them in popularity. Only a few species are sold, but these are larger (to four or five inches) heavily frilled species usually tinted in red or yellow. One valve is firmly attached to the bottom, so good specimens often come complete with the rock or decayed shell they were attached to. Large, colorful specimens of *Chama lazarus* make attractive conversation pieces.

The remaining bivalves (there are about 20,000 species) could be broken into just a few groups indicating collector interests: giant clams, cockles, brightly colored species, and oddly shaped species. Giant clams, *Tridacna* and *Hippopus,* are rather roundly triangular shells that are white in color or sometimes variegated with red and brown. They are most famous for the large size of most of the few species, some of which have actually been used as baptismal fonts and can usually be found displayed in curio shop windows. Juvenile shells are attractive and manageable, so they are rather popular. Cockles or cardiums, family Cardiidae, are a diversified family of small to quite large clams found in both cold and tropical waters. Although many species are plain brown, others are yellow, red, or pleasantly variegated, many are spined, and a few—such as heart cockles—are oddly shaped. If any other family of bivalves rivals the pectens in popularity, it must be the cockles.

Numerous species in many families are attractive shades of pink, violet, yellow, and other nice colors combined with either attractive sculpturing or smooth and glossy shells. Chief among these are species of *Tellina,* the tellins, *Donax,* the coquinas, and various lucinids. Many venus clams, family Venereidae, are glossy and nicely sculptured, so they have a certain degree of popularity, especially species of *Sunetta, Tapes,* and *Lioconcha.* The wedding cake venus, *Bassina,* has heavy transverse sharp ribs that look like delicate pink icing on a white shell, while some species of *Pitar* have long spines at one edge.

Bizarrely shaped shells occur in many families, including delicate mud-burrowing angelwings (several genera), strap-like razor clams (again several genera and families), and bizarre watering can or sprinkler clams where the minute valves are barely visible and the long calcareous tube developed around the siphons ends in a perforated "sprinkler head." None of these shells are really expensive, and a very attractive collection can be formed with ease—if you have the space to house it.

ODDS AND ENDS

The remaining molluscan marine groups are extremely marginal with collectors. Monoplacs *(Neopilina)* are deep-sea limpet-like shells distinguished by details of the animal from true gastropods; as far as I know few or none are in private hands

Some unusual shells. 1) Whole and bisected shells of the chambered nautilus, *Nautilus pompilius.* 2) The egg cradle of a paper nautilus, *Argonauta,* a "shell" secreted by the arms of the octopus-like animal. 3) An articulated set of the cleaned shell segments (sometimes called butterfly shells) of a chiton. 4) An uncleaned pen or cuttlebone of the primitive squid *Sepia.* Photos 1-3 by Ken Lucas, Steinhart Aquarium; photo 4 by G. Marcuse.

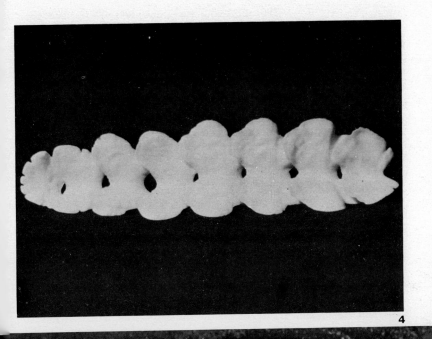

4

(most are extremely small anyway), and none have been offered by dealers. If available, the interest would probably be great as these shells have a reputation (perhaps undeserved) as "living fossils."

Tusk shells or elephant-tooth shells, Scaphopoda, are a bit more collectable. Most species are very small, white, greatly elongated shells open at both ends, but a few species, especially some from Japanese waters, are greenish or violet, heavily ribbed, and may reach six inches in length. Five or ten large species are commonly offered by dealers.

Chitons (Polyplacophora) have a small group of devotees and are offered by dealers more often than the other groups mentioned above. Their main disadvantages are several, including generally small size, dull colors, segmented shells that require rather complicated cleaning procedures, and the absence of collector literature on the group as a whole. A few dozen larger species (one inch or more) from the East Pacific, Japan, and Australia are offered by dealers, but this is only a small fraction of the nearly one thousand species, most of which are found in cooler waters.

The cephalopods (octopus, squid, etc.) offer little to collectors as most lack any type of real shell. The cuttlefishes (*Sepia* and allies) have a rather large internal shell, but I know of little collector interest in them and have never seen one offered for sale, although they are not uncommon in beach drift of the Mediterranean and Australian areas. One small squid, *Spirula,* has a delicate coiled buoyant internal shell that is deposited on beaches around the world and occasionally appears on lists as an oddity. The delicate sculptured egg cases (not really shells) of the paper nautiluses, *Argonauta* (a type of octopus), have a good market although the species are practically impossible to distinguish.

The only cephalopod shell that really enters the collector market is that of the few species of *Nautilus,* the only living members of the group with an external shell. The beautiful shells of the chambered nautiluses are whitish with reddish flammules posteriorly. When treated with chemicals in a process called pearlizing, the brown and white outer layer can be removed to reveal the glistening mother-of-pearl undershell. When split down the middle the chambers are visible as is the gas tube that causes flotation. Most collections probably have a nautilus shell or two in them for general interest and beauty. The common eight-inch Philippine species *(Nautilus pompilius)* generally sells for under $10, but the other two or three species are considerably more expensive.

THE NEW FRONTIER

Late in the last century and early in this one, land snails were popular with many collectors and were staples on the lists of dealers. Some brought very high prices for the day, and dealers and private collectors actually hired native collectors by the month or year to do nothing but collect land snails in the Philippines, South America, Australia, Fiji, etc. After World War I the interest in land snails for some reason almost disappeared, and only recently has interest begun to return. Land snails are a diverse group of many families, are usually small snails (the ones collected averaging from about half an inch to two or three inches in length), and generally are shades of brown although some are more brightly colored. (The colors of many species are in the periostracum, so never put a land snail in Clorox.®) The pleasure in collecting them comes from interest in their delicate tones, sometimes odd shapes, and the exotic countries from which they come. Most are tropical and closely associated with trees (some feed on the tree itself, others on fungi living on the tree), so the most collectable species are often called tree snails.

The most easily available land snails, and certainly the most popular, are the Florida and Caribbean tree snails, *Liguus*. These relatively large (usually over one inch long) and nicely elongated tree snails come in many colors, usually with darker bands on light backgrounds. Only three or four species are commonly available, but there are many named varieties varying in price from $1 to $50 or more. Smaller Hawaiian equivalents of *Liguus* are the achatinellas, which are often sinistral (the mouth or aperture opens on the left side rather than the usual right). Many of these have been extinct for years and bring relatively high prices. The southern Asian species of *Amphidromus* are also very similar to *Liguus* and quite popular.

The gigantic Philippine genus *Helicostyla* varies in shape from

conical to depressed, in size from less than an inch to over four inches, and in color from solid brown to solid yellow. No one knows how many species there are, because taxonomists once tended to name almost every shell as a new species, but at least forty or fifty supposed species are available for under $5 each.

Other popular land snails are the snake-patterned Asian *Cyclophorus,* the delicate New Guinea *Papuina,* the graceful but plainly colored Australasian *Placostylus,* the large Brazilian *Strophocheilus,* and the ear-shaped Brazilian *Auris* and *Zaplagius.* The range of collectable shells is limited only by the imagination, as there are several thousand possible species large enough to be of interest to collectors.

If land snails never regain their old popularity, it will be for a combination of two reasons. First, they are practically impossible to identify. Much of the taxonomy is based on internal anatomy, so it is difficult to put shells in the proper family, let alone genus. Most of the taxonomic literature is over 50 years old and much of it is at least 100. The concept of species has changed drastically since then and much of the old literature is more expensive and harder to obtain than the shells, plus practically worthless.

The second reason is that live land snails are closely associated with tropical forests, and forests are disappearing at a very rapid rate. Many of the shells sold today were taken 50 or more years ago from populations that no longer exist, especially in the case of Hawaiian tree snails. Florida tree snails are now found mostly in isolated "islands" of their food trees in localities that are often closely guarded secrets. As the forests of Brazil, the Philippines, Indonesia, and New Guinea are cut for timber and to clear farmland, the snails disappear with the trees. In many cases snails whose exact origins are unknown may have become extinct without ever being seen alive by collectors, and even once-common snails like the Manus Island green tree snail are considered endangered. The shells are nice, but if demand increases, where will the material come from?

Facing page: A group of tropical land snails showing the diversity of shapes and patterns available to collectors at the moment. Photo by Richard Goldberg, Worldwide Specimen Shells.

A minute selection of the available conchological literature. Photos by Glen S. Axelrod.

*Reading
is
Fundamental*

It is my emphatic belief that any collector above the level of complete tyro must also collect literature. This is an inescapable necessity if you are to protect yourself against misidentifications, learn of new shells, learn of changes of opinions in the classification of shells, and learn of the diversity of shells available for the collection. Books and more ephemeral publications are worth as much as the shells—and never let anyone convince you otherwise. A few dollars invested wisely could save you many dollars over the years and increase your enjoyment of the hobby manyfold.

In the last ten years or so the amount of technical and semi-technical literature available to collectors has inceased significantly. A typical dealer's catalog specializing in in-print

Three Pacific murexes. 1) *Murex pecten.* 2) *Chicoreus artemis.* 3) *Siratus pliciferoides.* Dealers list almost all murexes under the convenient genus *Murex.* From *Shells of Japan* by T. Okutani, Kodansha Publishers.

A few conchs of unusual form. 1) *Tibia insulaechorab,* a common tibia. 2) *Strombus listeri,* an elegant species with a large "wing." 3 & 4) *Lambis violacea,* a beautiful and expensive spider conch. Photos by the author.

conchological and malacological books and papers lists over 250 titles varying in price from $1 to over $100. Unfortunately the cheaper publications are becoming fewer each year because of the continual increases in printing costs and the greater emphasis on color in modern publications. With few exceptions, you pretty much get what you pay for in a book. The following pages will attempt to list and comment on just a very small sampling of literature available to collectors—it's barely possible to even scratch the surface of the literature field. Because of increasing prices I'll only attempt a rough guide to prices as follows: E-expensive, over $30; M-moderate, about $10 to $30; and C-cheap, under $10.

PERIODICALS

Included here are both amateur-oriented publications and scientific journals. Lately the line between these two groups has grown fuzzy, but this seems to be to the collector's advantage.

Hawaiian Shell News (Hawaiian Malacological Society, P.O. Box 10391, Honolulu, Hawaii 96816) is a slender monthly with a great deal of reader input, perhaps too much at times. It is the leading American club publication and probably the best for keeping up with recent discoveries in shells, dealer ads, book reviews, etc.; well illustrated. (M)

Of Sea and Shore (P.O. Box 33, Port Gamble, Washington 98364) is directed more to the real amateur collector and beachcomber than is *HSN,* with more accounts of collecting trips, articles on non-molluscs such as sea urchins or whales, and many ads. Printing quality is not as good as *HSN,* but fairly satisfactory. (C)

La Conchiglia (Via C. Federici, 1-00147, Rome, Italy) is perhaps the most interesting and useful foreign publication, but it must be remembered that some of its scientific articles are considered a bit unusual by American standards. Currently it features a continuing series of articles on the rarer cowries, and in the recent past it has had long series on the conchs and European pectens. English language edition; bimonthly; heavily illustrated in color. (M) (Pay for the air mail postage—the envelope will not stand the rigors of sea mail shipment, thus lost magazines.)

The Veliger (California Malacozoological Society, 1584 Milvia St., Berkeley, California 94709) is a thick quarterly of strictly scientific appeal. Although it publishes a few papers each year that deal with collectable shells, the content is heavily slanted toward obscure gastropods and bivalves and the nudibranchs. It is probably best to just check it in your local college library once or twice a year. (M)

The Nautilus (American Malacologists, P.O. Box 2255, Melbourne, Florida 32901) is the oldest American molluscan publication. A rather slim quarterly, its papers tend to emphasize land and freshwater molluscs, but mostly the obscure types; many new species descriptions. Check it in your library. (M)

There are numerous other club and scientific publications available, and many are very good. Most are rather restricted in their area of interest, either geographically or through subject content, and are probably of only occasional interest to the average collector.

GENERAL BOOKS

This is a very large category including both cheap paperbacks and expensively produced volumes on specific areas.

In the very general or introductory class fall such volumes as *Seashells of the World* by R.T. Abbott and *Sea Shells* by S.P. Dance (both C), heavily illustrated paperbacks readily available in almost any good bookstore. Between them they cover most major groups of molluscs and give the beginner a good grasp of the variation in the entire phylum. Essential and worth the few dollars.

The Collector's Encyclopedia of Shells by S.P. Dance, *Field Guide to Seashells of the World* by G. Linder (both M), and *Guide to Shells* by A.P.H. Oliver (C) are good guides for the general collector as they illustrate many hundreds of the most common and collectable shells with brief descriptions. In a somewhat different vein is *Standard Catalog of Shells* by Wagner and Abbott (E), a thick loose-leaf volume that attempts to list the collectable shells of the world with values. Unfortunately the current edition has many faults, not least of which is a wildly unrealistic pricing guide that is misleading to collectors. Buy it if you must, but I can't really recommend it except to specialists.

A few typical conchs. Top row (left to right): *Strombus lentiginosus, S. aratrum;* bottom row: *S. variabilis, S. gibberulus, S. vittatus.* Photo by K. Gillett.

Triton's trumpet, *Charonia tritonis*. From *Shells of Japan* by T. Okutani, Kodansha Publishers.

In the geographical coverage books are numerous volumes of sometimes only marginal interest to collectors (few European shells enter into most collections, for instance) and some that are almost essential. In the essential category fall *Shells of New Guinea and the Central Indo-Pacific* by A. Hinton (M), *Marine Shells of the Pacific*, volumes 1 and 2, by W.O. Cernohorsky (M), and *Tropical Pacific Marine Shells*, also by Cernohorsky (E). These four volumes together cover the majority of all collectable Indo-Pacific shells likely to enter the general collection and are heavily illustrated with photographs. They are of interest to specialists because of their extensive coverage of the major families from this area and are essential to the general collector.

The Australian area has produced several good books heavily illustrated in color, the best being *Australian Shells* by Wilson and Gillett (unfortunately out of print). Several new Australian books are coming onto the market at this time, including a heavily illustrated field guide to Australian shells; check with your dealer for further information.

Japan has produced many heavily illustrated color books of shells of both northern and tropical waters, but they have the disadvantages of being extremely expensive at the moment and having only meager written descriptions that are translated (often poorly) from the Japanese. Perhaps the best available is the two-volume *Shells of the Western Pacific in Color* by Kira and Habe (watch out—several different editions from 1960 to the mid-1970's are available, often with different names for the same shells), but it may cost you $100 for a set. *Sea Shells of Sagami Bay* by Kuroda and others is a massive book dealing with the cooler Japanese fauna and featuring mostly shells of no collector interest; at $115 or more its price tag is also massive. The several cheap paperbacks on Japanese shells are virtually useless for identifications.

Hawaii is the center for SCUBA collectors and probably hosts the most active group of collectors in the world. There are several good cheap little paperbacks on the more familiar Hawaiian shells, including *Hawaiian Seashells* by Quirk and Harrison, but the large and heavily illustrated *Hawaiian Marine Shells* by E.A. Kay is the current manual for advanced collectors and covers many shells found in other parts of the Pacific (M).

I know of no good books giving more than a casual treatment of the shells of the Indian Ocean, not even the "hot" collecting areas such as the Red Sea, Thailand, or India, and even the coasts of Africa are very poorly represented by literature. To identify a shell from these areas you just have to hope it is included in a Pacific book or go to the more technical literature. A modern guide to shells of South Africa is being prepared at the time of writing, and another guide to shells of the Oman area should be available soon; again, check with your book dealer.

As the European interest in shelling in western African countries continues to grow, there are sure to be comprehensive books on this area made available. A few small books already exist for a few countries.

The tropical eastern Pacific is handsomely covered by M. Keen's *Seashells of Tropical West America* (M), an over 1,000-page manual with virtually every species illustrated in black and white.

Field Guide to the Shells of the Atlantic and Gulf Coasts and *Field Guide to the Shells of the Pacific Coast and Hawaii*, both by P. Morris (C-M) are barely adequate but easily available manuals covering the more familiar shells of the United States coasts proper. The plates are crowded and few reliable characters are given to really help identify the shells, but many species are covered. *Seashells of North America* by R.T. Abbott (C) is a color-illustrated paperback that adequately covers the common shells of both coasts. Several local-interest manuals are available covering the shells of northwestern Canada, the Pacific Northwest generally, California, the Northeast, and Texas. Florida has numerous books on its fauna, from very cheap paperbacks of most interest to tourists to moderately priced manuals quite useful to the advanced collector. The "daddy" of all American books is *American Seashells* by R.T. Abbott (E), 1974 edition, which attempts to cover the seashells of both American coasts and the Caribbean-East Pacific areas as well. Many species are illustrated in color and black and white, but the treatment per species is often scanty as might be expected of a book that covers 6,000 shells. *Caribbean Seashells* by Warmke and Abbott (C) is an excellent guide to Puerto Rico and vicinity though a bit outdated now. *Sea Shells of the West Indies* by M. Humfrey (M) gives a

Some Pacific cymatids. 1) *Fusitriton oregonensis.* 2) *Turritriton tenuliratum.* 3) *Distorsio reticulata.* 4) *Biplex perca.* From *Shells of Japan* by T. Okutani, Kodansha Publishers.

74

Common Indo-Pacific helmet shells. 1 & 2) Variations of *Phalium bisulcatum*. 3) *Phalium flammiferum*. 4) *Casmaria ponderosa*. From *Shells of Japan* by T. Okutani, Kodansha Publishers.

more modern coverage, especially of the southern Caribbean, as does *Shells of the Caribbean* by J.B. Lozet (C).

The Atlantic coast of South America has few shell books available, not even for the now more heavily collected Venezuelan area. The best I know of are *Coastal Brazilian Seashells* (M) and *Brazilian Marine Mollusks Iconography* (M) by E. Rios, but both are little more than poorly illustrated lists. I understand a guide to South American shells is now in preparation.

European shells tend to be dull brownish things with usually little interest to American collectors, but they are of course popular in European countries and with some specialists. There are many books on European marine shells, but many are in foreign languages and thus of little utility to the average American collector. You might try *British Shells* by N.F. McMillan (C) for an introduction to the fauna or the *Carta d'Identita della Conchiglie del Mediterraneo* by P. Parenzan, a four-part Italian guide to Mediterranean shells (E).

SPECIALIZED BOOKS

Books on the taxonomy and identification of specific groups of shells are as old as the hobby. The old literature of the 19th and early 20th centuries is usually available only in specialized libraries as they are collector's items originally printed in very small numbers and often destroyed to obtain the beautiful colored plates that made them famous. Such authors as Reeve, Sowerby, Kiener, and Tryon attempted to cover all the shells of the world in many volumes, with of course emphasis on the collectable shells. These works, called iconographies, are as a general rule not available to the average collector and are probably of little practical value to him either.

Books on the major families are becoming more common again, although they are often controversial, are expensive, and are never the last word in identification or taxonomy. The experienced collector understands that every book merely reflects the opinions of the author or authors and will eventually be superseded by another and hopefully better book. With this in mind, I'll mention a few of the modern references on the major families and other groups.

Cones: I'm not too modest, so I'll start with my own *Cone Shells: A Synopsis of the Living Conidae* (M). This work attempts to describe and illustrate in color every living species of cone and their major varieties. The emphasis is where it should be in a work of this type, comparison of different species to allow the collector to identify his shells with some confidence.

Cowries: Cowry collectors are fortunate to have two good but quite different books available. *Cowries (Second Edition)* by yours truly (M) is a simplified account of the living species with emphasis on identification and enlarged color photos of every species. There is an up-to-date pricing guide (as in *Cone Shells* also), a full index of synonyms, and a synopsis of subspecies and varieties. *The Living Cowries* by C.M. Burgess (E, out of print) is a large-format volume with numerous color plates and more discussions, though it often fails to differentiate similar species; a new edition or supplement is being prepared. Both books should be on the shelf of every cowry collector.

Cowry Allies: Three recent scientific revisions by C.N. Cate are available from dealers and cover virtually all the allies: *Systematic Revision of the . . . Ovulidae; Review of the Triviidae;* and *Review of the Eratoidae* (M). These are useful for the numerous photos, but the taxonomy is confusing and often obscures identification by placing very similar species in different genera.

Volutes: The standard reference is the sumptuous *The Living Volutes* by Weaver and duPont (E). An excellent treatment of the family, it is gorgeously illustrated but now a bit outdated. Still useful for its study of variation is *Multiform Australian Volutes* by F. Abbottsmith (M); most collectable volutes are Australian in origin, so this remains an essential volume.

Murexes: The recently published *Murex Shells of the World* by Radwin and D'Attilio (E) is perhaps the most modern reference, but it has numerous problems for the collector such as minute photos of small species, lack of comparisons, and an unwieldly generic classification that makes it virtually impossible to use. I find it easier to use *The Murex Book* by R. Fair (C), which is not as scientific and lacks color but is well illustrated and more useful for general reference. Neither book is complete, however.

Conchs: The new *Conchs, Tibias, and Harps* by yours truly

Marine snails come in many shapes and colors, as illustrated by the small assortment shown above. 1) *Ninella.* 2) *Cypraea.* 3) *Nassarius.* 4) *Conus.* 5) *Phalium.* 6) *Dicathais.* 7) *Janthina.* 8) *Bellastraea.* 9) *Subninella.* 10) *Struthiolaria.* 11) *Mitra.* 12) *Cronia.* 13) *Conuber.* 14) *Dinassovica.* Photo by K. Gillett of Australian shells.

A few interesting bivalves. 1) *Amusium balloti.* 2) *Laciolina quoyi.* 3) *Trisidos tortuosa.* 4) *Gloripallium pallium.* 5) *Fragum unedo.* 6) *Lioconcha castrensis.* 7) *Regozara flava.* 8) *Tapes literata.* Photo by K. Gillett of Australian species.

again (C) covers all the species of the Strombidae and throws in the Harpidae as well. (Why such different shells in one book? I happen to like harps and they served to nicely fill in the book and make it a better value.) Fully illustrated in color, the emphasis is again on identification. Range maps help in recognition of subspecies.

Olives: Olive Shells of the World by Zeigler and Porreca (M) is an adequate coverage of the genus *Oliva* but lacks any coverage of the allies; there is also an over-emphasis on varieties that is frustrating to collectors. A more comprehensive work is said to be in preparation.

Miters: Mitridae of the World, Part 1, by W.O. Cernohorsky (E) covers the subfamily Mitrinae, which has a good number of collectable species. *Systematics of the Families Mitridae and Volutomitridae* by Cernohorsky (M) covers the genera.

Bivalves: There are very few books on bivalves, not even the pectens, which are almost impossible to identify. Three volumes of *Treatise on Invertebrate Paleontology* edited by R.C. Moore (E) give a comprehensive treatment of living and fossil genera, but most collectors will find them too expensive and technical to use. *Panamic–Pacific Pelecypoda* by A. Olsson (M) is a heavily illustrated coverage of the East Pacific species but is again very technical. Some general books have some coverage of bivalves, but none are even nearly complete. *British Bivalve Seashells* by N. Tebble is a good introduction to the European species.

Land Snails: Alas, there is no really good book on land snails available. Webb's *Foreign Land Snails* (M) is interesting as it illustrates many shells (in heavily retouched black and white), but the identifications are very, very poor and the book is over 30 years old. *Guide to Shells of Papua New Guinea* by A. Hinton (M) illustrates several dozen New Guinea land snails in color, but this is only a drop in the bucket. Florida tree snails were well covered and illustrated in an article in the March, 1965, issue of *National Geographic Magazine. The Shell Makers* by A. Solem (M) is an excellent introduction to land and freshwater molluscs, with beautiful scanning electron microscope photos. Most land snail literature is very old, very technical, or both.

Miscellaneous: Three books don't quite fit any of the above classifications. The first is *Kingdom of the Seashell* by R.T. Abbott (M), which is an excellent introduction to the molluscs as a whole, combining information on the living animals with information on the better known shells; a classic. *Rare Shells* by S.P. Dance (M, out of print) is a classic study of several of the rarest shells including color photos of many type specimens. The value of the book lies in its photos, the interesting discussions of the histories of the specimens, and comparison with the current status of many shells once known only from a specimen or two and now familiar on almost every dealer's list. Finally, *Handbuch der Systematischen Weichtierkunde* by J. Thiele is the last comprehensive survey of the living molluscs, attempting to describe and illustrate every genus known in the early part of the century. This is still the only available reference for many groups of shells. Written in German and very technical, the reprint currently sells for about $100, so it is obviously of interest and use only to advanced collectors and libraries.

A beach specimen of *Aporrhais pespelicani*, the European pelican's-foot; such poor specimens are usually sold as commercial shells and do not enter the specimen-grade market. Photo by G. Marcuse.

Good shelling areas are becoming difficult to find. Reefs like those of the Tuamotus (above) and the Maldives (right) are difficult to reach and often protected by local regulations. Photo above by J. Jaubert (courtesy Nancy Aquarium), that at right by Dr. Herbert R. Axelrod.

The Environmental Question

The last decade has seen the rise of the "environmentalist generation" and an increasing number of questions being asked about the value and possible harm of any type of natural history collecting. Shell collecting has not been harassed as badly as hunting, fishing, butterfly collecting, or cactus collecting, but it does have its detractors. In a few instances shell shows have been picketed by poorly informed environmentalists or even cancelled because of political pressure. In many schools shell collections are frowned upon as giving youths the wrong idea about how to enjoy nature. A few small countries have begun to strictly regulate shell collecting in their waters, probably wisely so, and California and Florida have taken steps in that direction.

There is no doubt that some types of shell collecting *do* endanger local populations of a few species, but it is doubtful if any collectable shell (*i.e.,* species of the major families such as cones, cowries, and volutes) is currently endangered by collecting practices, though there are a few cases where limited range and heavy collecting pressure may lead to a species' destruction if steps are not taken.

Before going further, a distinction must be made between specimen collecting and commercial collecting. Specimen collecting centers on taking the best possible specimens of shells that are wanted by collectors. The tendency is of course to collect, clean, and offer for sale only species that have a ready market or look different enough to perhaps be of interest to collectors. Juveniles and brooding females are seldom or never collected, and badly broken or deformed living specimens are ignored because of their token value. By this definition specimen collecting can only include types of collecting where living molluscs or recently dead ones are found by a collector and there is an element of choice—the specimen can be collected or left in the field. With the advent of SCUBA diving and its increased availability to collectors, it is now possible for diving clubs to actually over-collect an area and in a few cases even depopulate a small reef or sand flat. Fortunately, however, specimen collecting is more easily regulated by local governments if necessary and most collectors have enough sense to regulate themselves without government interference. Only by leaving the habitat intact and taking only as many shells as required will they have shells left for another day.

Beach collecting, the picking up of dead shells in collectable condition from the beach or very shallow water, probably has no effect at all on populations of marine animals. Although dead shells do contribute to the marine environment either as substrates for other animals or through return of their mineral content to the water, the few specimens picked up on a beach are meaningless compared to the number of shells that die each day from natural causes—or the millions that die from silting due to dredging of harbors and channels. At a beach-collecting Mecca like Sanibel Island, Florida, it is possible for the vast number of collectors (usually of the casual type) to actually outnumber the fresh shells found on a beach on any particular day, unless recent channel dredging has caused a die-off of local shells.

Commercial collecting is broader in scope and includes any activity where all molluscs available are collected, whether living or dead, juvenile or adult, valuable or unmarketable. In my opinion, this is the only type of collecting that can cause significant damage to a species. Collecting of molluscs by dredging, trawling, use of deep nets, or trapping is totally non-selective. Many of the rarest shells are taken by these techniques and are the ones that should cause some soul-searching among collectors.

Molluscs taken in trawling operations are usually the by-products of fishing fleets operating in deeper waters. The Taiwanese are especially proficient in making sure any mollusc taken in fishing trawls reaches a dealer and eventually a collector. The majority of shells taken in this way are already dead or die before the nets reach the vessel's decks. Juveniles are seldom taken, so it is doubtful that any but the largest shells can be seriously threatened by normal trawling operations. A few studies seem to indicate that trawling does relatively little damage to the bottom environment. Additionally, trawlers dislike rocky areas that lead to torn nets and lost tackle, so relatively few areas are subject to trawling pressure.

Dredging is an expensive proposition requiring specially modified vessels, a great deal of patience, and a good knowledge of the sea bottoms being fished. It is usually practiced only by scientific expeditions and a few die-hard collectors that make relatively little impact on the fauna, though commercial dredging for precious corals is practiced in a few areas. Dredging does take juveniles, however, and possibly causes more damage to the environment than does trawling, but only if practiced on a large scale as in coral dredging or suction dreding for commercial shells in large quantities. Again, relatively few living molluscs are taken in this way.

The growing use of nets set in deep water in the Philippines has produced specimens of numerous rare shells, but one must wonder about the ecological impact of a system that haphazardly removes living adult molluscs from their environment in large quantities in very restricted areas. The Philippines still practices an ancient and totally debunked hunting philosophy when it

Attractive Australian bivalves. 1) *Bassina sidneyensis.* 2) *Hemicardium hemicardium.* 3) *Solen correctus.* 4) *Tellina roseola.* 5) *Neotrigonia margaritacea.* 6) *Veletuceta flammea.* 7) *Austrolima nimbifer.* 8) *Fulvia racketti.* 9) *Musculus cumingianus.* 10) *Plebidonax deltoides.* 11) *Striacallista disrupta.* Photo by K. Gillett.

Two common cephalopod shells. 1) *Argonauta nodosa.* 2) *Nautilus pompilius,* with the preserved animal removed from the shell. Photos by Ken Lucas, Steinhart Aquarium.

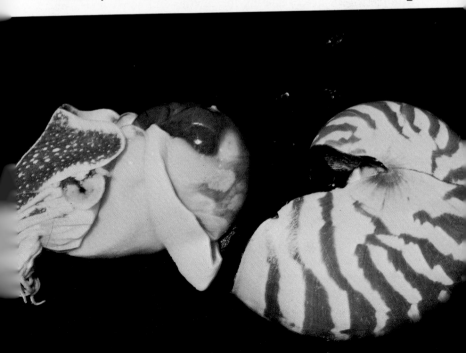

comes to shells: remove everything that might possibly be salable in whatever quantity available until it is no longer economically worthwhile to work an area for the few survivors, then move on to a new area. This philosophy results in quantities of practically worthless, flawed shells, as the net collectors place almost the same value on all specimens of a species regardless of condition; to them a subadult *Conus gloriamaris* with gigantic reef breaks is worth about the same as the one-in-a-hundred gem adult. The large quantity of specimens taken leads to a decrease in market value for uncommon species, which means the net collector has to try to take even more specimens to make a living. When an area is "fished-out" the collector moves to a new area without really caring if there is still a viable breeding population of molluscs left behind.

One net collector or one coral dredger does little damage, but dozens working in an area month after month must have serious effects on molluscs. The same is true of any type of large-scale collecting, whether by conch boats in the Bahamas, children wading for olives and common cowries in Kenya, or organized groups of skin divers looking for cowries and cones in Hawaii. Very few shells are greatly localized in distribution, attractive to collectors, *and* readily available to collectors. Only when this combination of variables exists is a shell in real trouble. Possible examples of shells that may face a crisis in the coming years include:

Cypraea cervus, a large cowry that is virtually restricted to Florida and the Bahamas and is under extreme pressure from collectors and land developers;

Cypraea teulerei, a once-rare cowry known from only a few localities in the Oman area and possibly being over-collected;

Conus nobilis, an uncommon cone with only a few scattered populations known and all the accessible populations being heavily collected; and

Oliva porphyria, the largest olive, which, though widely distributed on the Pacific Central American coast, is collected whenever it is found.

The rarer species, such as the glory-of-the-seas cone (*Conus gloriamaris*) and golden cowry (*Cypraea aurantium*), may be locally over-collected but have large ranges and are not easily

Cypraea cervus, a large and possibly threatened cowry.

subject to extensive collecting at the moment over the entire range.

I know of no adequate study on the type of commerical collecting that removes thousands of large shells from an area each year to be converted into lamp bases, napkin rings, and cute little carved objects. Fortunately this is not directly related to true shell collecting, but it is an excess that does tend to give shell collecting a bad reputation through association.

My experience is that over a third of all shells offered by dealers to specimen collectors were dead when collected. They may have been cleaned up a bit to look almost live-taken, but they were really freshly dead when collected or are the by-products of regulated trawling operations and would have been removed from the population anyway. The taking of such specimens probably has no real effect on the environment, and neither does the selective taking of a few living adults by a few collectors at any locality. The only possibility of real damage comes when many collectors work in a restricted area, either taking anything available or specializing in one or a few valuable species. The very number of collectors has to lead to some damage to the environment.

The future promises more marine parks with no or limited collecting and more careful regulation of collecting in populated areas. There is no reason why shell collecting cannot be

90

Pleurotomaria hirasei, one of the more common Japanese slit shells, shown about natural size. From *Shells of Japan* by T. Okutani, Kodansha Publishers.

Opposite:
A diversity of shells. 1) *Sepia rex*, the internal shell of a cuttlefish. 2) *Cypraea labrolineata*, a cowry. 3) *Patellanax perplexa*, a limpet. 4) *Dentalium lubricatum*, a tusk shell. 5) *Spirula spirula*, the internal shell of a small squid. 6) *Pterynotus angasi*, a murex shell. 7) *Haliotis ruber*, an abalone. 8) *Morula marginalba*, a "typical" snail. Photo by K. Gillett.

Shell collectors all have an effect on the marine environment, no matter how they collect. The effect may be minimal, as in beach collecting (above), or drastic, as in systematic SCUBA collecting (below), but it exists. Only by carefully regulating their personal collecting habits can collectors prevent governmental licensing and restrictive regulations. Photo above by Dr. Herbert R. Axelrod, that below by Dr. L.P Zann.

Without corals, many shells could not survive. One of the first duties of every collector is to protect the living corals at all costs. Photo by R. Scheer.

regulated and licensed like trout fishing or deer hunting, with the fees going to improve or repair the collecting habitat. Underdeveloped countries are unlikely to be able to afford complicated licensing schemes for many years, especially when a sizable part of their income results directly or indirectly from shells. The disturbing trend of closing entire countries or areas to collecting is only a partial answer to the problem, for it does not provide for any means of improving the habitat to bring reduced mollusc populations back to their former numbers and also means a loss of revenue to divers and others who pay taxes to the governments concerned.

LAST WORDS

Well, I've come to the end of my allotted pages and find I still haven't covered several topics I wanted to mention, such as speculation in shells (don't, unless you can afford to get badly burned), taxonomy (almost a book by itself and probably too technical to fit here anyway), and shell stamps (several good books are now available on this growing hobby). I hope I've answered some of your questions and given you some ideas about how to collect and what to collect. Remember that whether you spend only a few dollars a year on your hobby or thousands, a hobby exists for your enjoyment. Happy collecting!

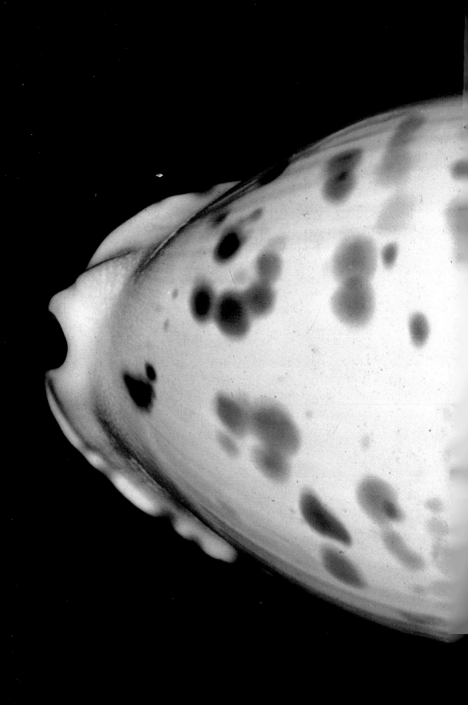